SUCCESS IN YOUR NEW MISSION

A Guide for Senior Military Leaders in Transition

VERA STEINER BLORE

SUCCESS IN YOUR NEW MISSION: A Guide for Senior
Military Leaders in Transition
Copyright © 2014 by Vera Steiner Blore. All rights reserved.
ISBN 978-0-9915613-0-8

To Ted, who provided the spark for this book and
to Rob, who is the reason I wrote it.

ACKNOWLEDGEMENTS

This book would not have been possible without the encouragement, wisdom and mentorship provided by several individuals. The first is my long-time mentor, colleague and friend, Roz Stark, who not only edited the manuscript, but has supported me through several key life transitions.

I also am very grateful to my colleague, Jim Carman, retired Navy Captain and currently the Military Officers Association of America (MOAA) Director of Career Transition Services, who continues to be an invaluable source of transition wisdom.

Vince Patton, the eighth Master Chief Petty Officer of the U.S. Coast Guard and currently Vice President, Homeland Security Programs at the Armed Forces Communications and Electronics Association (AFCEA), also has shared great insight with me and continues to lend his support to senior enlisted personnel in transition to civilian life.

I am equally indebted to the retired senior military leaders who have been willing to share their own transition experiences, both in conversation and through interviews featured in *Military Leaders in Transition* (www.seniormilitaryintransition.com). These individuals demonstrate their continued leadership by acknowledging that, while the path ahead is not always straightforward or readily apparent, it can be successfully navigated. While many had input into this publication, I am solely responsible for any errors or unintentional misstatements.

Finally, I am most grateful to my husband, Gary, and to our children, David and Anna, for riding the rollercoaster of life's ups and downs together as a family.

INTRODUCTION

Many might wonder why making the transition from senior military status to civilian life would be difficult. After all, these executives have demonstrated leadership, marshaled vast human and financial resources, and provided vision and strategy to achieve key objectives. Military leaders have moved dozens of times during their careers - frequently overseas - and, in some cases, took on life-or-death missions. Surely putting on a suit, mastering the art of the interview, and learning about profit-and-loss statements can't be *that* difficult...

In reality, several factors complicate the transition process for senior military leaders. Stepping back into civilian life after decades within the military social structure often presents surprising obstacles. These include:

- Adapting to a significant career shift at a not-so-young age;

- Experiencing a disorienting loss of identity, purpose and mission;

- Confronting the reality of your "market value" in today's job market compared to your civilian and military competition;

- Adapting to a different workplace culture in which your new boss may be the same age as your son or daughter;

- Acknowledging a need for help after a long career in which "handling things" on one's own was expected.

Add to this the loss of a team whose bonds have grown stronger through shared work and life experiences, and it is no wonder that many senior leaders experience a sense of deep isolation as they step away from their lengthy military careers.

Having recently gone through this major life change in partnership with my husband and having transitioned my own career at least nine times over the course of our military life together, I have become a passionate advocate for improving how we prepare senior military members and their families for successful transition back into civilian life.

In 2012, I launched *Military Leaders in Transition,* an online forum (www.seniormilitaryintransition.com) to explore ways that military leaders, employers, recruiters, executive career consultants and family members can be better prepared to understand and address the diverse challenges faced by senior leaders reintegrating back into civilian life. Many transitioning military leaders are relieved to learn they are not alone in their struggles to adapt to a civilian job market they last experienced as teenagers.

While many excellent books have been written about the basics of transition from military service, they tend to put the emphasis on creating a resume void of military acronyms, ensuring an updated business wardrobe, and identifying best practices for job interviews. These are important components, but they represent only the tip of the iceberg. The underlying assumption is that senior military leaders should be able to independently figure out the rest of what they need to know to be successful in civilian life. That is an unrealistic expectation. This book intentionally adopts a different approach.

The advice shared in the following pages is drawn from online and personal interviews I've conducted as well as insights from other experts. This is not a treatise on resume writing or interview strategy; rather, I hope to shed light on a process that is too often oversimplified and taken for granted. This book is organized into three distinct sections:

- Stepping Out of Military Life
- Getting Ready for What Comes Next
- Activating Your Action Plan

Questions posed throughout the book are intended to provoke thought and introspection, as well as foster conversation with mentors, colleagues, friends and family who know you best. You also are encouraged to use the book's open spaces to brainstorm ideas and outline potential avenues of interest to you.

Successful military to civilian transition goes far beyond crafting a well-written resume or even landing a new job. It is about internal acceptance of a dramatic change in one's own self-image, identifying a new place to "belong" and finding a new passion and role in life. It is about redefining one's purpose and identity the day the uniform comes off. Looking in the mirror, the question is: Who am I and how do I figure out what comes next? While everyone's journey will be unique, the more you prepare, the better equipped you and your family will be to tackle this major life change with confidence and success.*

---

* This book is written for senior military officers and senior enlisted members in transition. While some of the guidance may be equally relevant to junior service members, the book's focus is on military careerists who are 40 to 60 years-old and are reentering civilian life.

CONTENTS

SECTION ONE
STEPPING OUT OF MILITARY LIFE

SECTION TWO
GETTING READY FOR WHAT COMES NEXT

SECTION THREE
ACTIVATING YOUR ACTION PLAN

HELPFUL RESOURCES

ALL IN THE MILITARY FAMILY

If someone had told me 30 years ago that I would one day consider myself part of the "military family" and ultimately struggle with separating from it, I would have assumed the person was hallucinating. Growing up in New York City, I had no direct contact with anyone in the military other than my father, who had served exactly one month before being honorably discharged during World War II, years before I was born.

As a political science major, I decided to write my senior thesis on the Carter Administration's decision not to produce the neutron bomb. This paper led to two years of post-college internships in Washington, D.C., focused on arms control and preventing nuclear war. My internship experiences locked in a misguided perspective that people in the military are without feelings, emotions or the capacity to think for themselves, whose leaders are solely focused on war-fighting and war-mongering.

Imagine my surprise on my first day of graduate school when I heard another student's voice boom in self-introduction: *"LT GARY THOMAS BLORE, SIR, U.S. COAST GUARD."* Lo and behold, there was a real military officer, sitting two rows in front of me in the classroom. I had never met one before.

I wasn't quite sure what to think of the lieutenant's presence. Why was he pursuing a graduate degree? My curiosity soon got the better of me. A few weeks into the semester, I saw Gary speaking with a classmate of ours at a school-sponsored event; he had the "audacity" to wear his military uniform. I decided it was time for action.

"So," I boldly said, "What do you think about nuclear war, anyway?" Gary calmly paused for a moment, looked me squarely in the eye, and said, "I am against it." This simplistic answer is exactly what I deserved in response to such an ignorant question, but at the time, it was also all I needed to hear. Apparently, there was far more to learn about those serving in the military than I previously thought...

Two years later, on graduation day, Gary and I were married. So began my real introduction to military life.

Unlike those military spouses who are former military members themselves or are children of military parents, I had little understanding of military life when we began our lives together. I was more interested in pursuing my own career and viewed involvement in military life as something of an obligation. As time passed, and with each successive move, I worked hard to advance my professional skills and maintain my own identity; I regularly reminded my civilian friends and colleagues that the military was my husband's life, not mine. After all, as far as I was concerned, I had only made a commitment of marriage to Gary; I later learned I had, at the same time, also entered into a long-term relationship with the military.

My understanding increased significantly about the military community's tight-knit fabric and cohesiveness as Gary moved into positions of greater responsibility. While my mother used to call ours a "gypsy lifestyle," I came to appreciate that it was the military's extensive formal and informal support network that made our frequent relocations feel feasible and sure-footed.

Every time military members, their spouses and children relocate for a new assignment, they get to meet and socialize with a different set of "relatives" in the broader "military family." While the geography changed with every move, Gary and I always remained part of a community into which we were readily welcomed and accepted. The local "family" is always ready to share recommendations about the best doctors, dentists, schools, hardware stores and hair salons in town. If one needs help getting settled in, there is no need to look far to find it.

When I learned in 2010 that my husband would face mandatory retirement after a 36-year military career, I was surprised at the impact this had on me. I had managed to advance my own career, had become adept at quickly making new friends and readily adjusted to new environments. Yet the news that our military life would soon draw to an end led to personal feelings of shock and disbelief. One might have thought I would have appreciated our new-found freedom – the ability to make choices about where to live, avoid the stress of another move based on someone else's decision and timeframe, and finally, to plant my own professional roots.

The truth is that, instead, I found myself walking around for months feeling only "semi-present" and though typically a Type-A, driven personality, I felt uncertain and unfocused. As someone who lived a kind of dual life, with one foot always engaged with the broader civilian community, I couldn't figure out why *Gary's* mandatory retirement left *me* feeling so strange and disconnected. And if I felt this way, I began to appreciate more fully the impact separation from military life would have on my own spouse and on other military colleagues reaching the end of their military careers.

The more I talked with others and wrote about this issue, the more I realized we were not alone. Speaking with other senior military colleagues and spouses, it became clear that we were not the only ones feeling uncertain about the future and lacking clarity about next steps. Many seemed to share our deep sense of loss. Having seen several of my husband's former colleagues still walking around with that glazed look in their eyes two or three years after their transition, I couldn't help wondering if they still wished they could trade their business suits for their old military uniforms.

*   *   *   *   *

PREPARING TO LEAVE "HOME"

Getting ready to leave one's professional and, in many respects, one's social "home" after a long military career is more complicated than it seems. In some ways, the process can be compared to a young person leaving home to live independently. Parents hope he or she will be able to draw on everything taught and learned while living at home and apply that knowledge successfully. They likely offer last minute reminders about the importance of staying focused, waking up on time and taking care of one's health, but in the end, it is up to the young person to head off and make the right choices. The longer one stays at home, the more difficult it can be to leave comforting and familiar surroundings.

Similarly, each of the individual military services offers brief transition workshops, though the quality and content varies. The brevity of these workshops precludes a deep dive into what it takes to complete a successful transition. Although the scope of the Transition Assistance Program (TAP) curriculum has been expanded for junior military personnel, more must be done to increase the preparedness of every military member heading into the civilian workforce.

Indeed, while basic TAP classes are being expanded, the U.S. Armed Services are cutting back on the availability of transition workshops for senior military executives. In spite of budget cutbacks, this makes little sense. Senior military leaders on active duty have not been in the civilian workforce since their teens; after 20 to 35 years in military service, most find themselves in unfamiliar territory when they retire. The longer one has served within the military, the harder it can be to move on successfully.

Executive Transition Assistance Programs (ETAP) must not only be retained in the face of shrinking federal budgets, but also must be brought up to date to reflect the realities of the current economy. All too often, ETAP courses provide only the most basic information, do not reflect current job search strategies or address some of the more complex aspects of a successful transition. These classes must include exploration of mental and physical readiness, balancing salary expectations versus passion for the new job, understanding the cultural and psychological aspects of the transition process and personal financial management as well as other critical topics.

Given the realities of budget cutbacks, senior military leaders must take ownership of their own transitions, take advantage of free and fee-based resources and workshops offered by well established professional associations, conduct the necessary research, and when desired, use the services of a consultant who can provide more customized support. These activities should be viewed as a sound investment with expected future dividends. Many career transition services are federally tax-deductible.

As an example, The Military Officers Association of America (MOAA) offers an array of helpful career transition services. MOAA's *Military Executives in Transition* (MET) workshop goes well beyond the content of traditional senior-level courses and includes one-on-one follow-on career transition consulting services as well. (Full disclosure: I have worked with MOAA on developing and presenting these workshops.)

Well before the last few weeks of their military careers, senior military leaders also must be encouraged and given the opportunity to research civilian career paths without being viewed as uninterested in further military advancement. Successful transition requires proactive thinking and planning; those forced to give the process short shrift at the end of their military careers often take the first job that comes along, no matter how poor the fit. The better prepared military leaders are to transition smoothly into the civilian marketplace, the greater respect that will accrue to them and, ultimately, to the services that readied them for continued success.

Transitioning senior military leaders have much to contribute to the workforce; society risks losing members from this significant talent pool who may opt to leave the workforce entirely rather than be forced to compete without adequate preparation.

*   *   *   *   *

SAYING GOODBYE...GRIEVING THE SEPARATION

Stoic though most will be when it is time to move on, leaving the military is a separation that can feel like losing a loved one. The military community is not only where you work and frequently live; it drives the type of work you do, sets the geographic parameters of where your children will attend school and where they will grow up. For some, separating from the military community is as major a life transition as getting married or losing a parent. While we may know intellectually that we eventually will leave military service, our hearts often take longer to accept this inevitability. The transition to civilian life also may be every bit as challenging for spouses who may struggle somewhat to adapt to a new reality.

Renowned psychiatrist Elisabeth Kubler-Ross wrote in her seminal book, *On Death and Dying*, about five stages in dealing with grief and loss. She noted that we do not necessarily experience these stages in linear order, nor will we necessarily experience all five.

The five phases are shock/denial, anger, bargaining, depression and acceptance.

In the *denial* phase, Kubler-Ross writes that many find themselves in a state of shock and denial about the loss. There is a feeling of numbness and individuals ask themselves how they will be able to move on.

Feeling *angry* suggests feeling pain inside and a perception that we have been deserted or abandoned – we are all alone.

Internally, we may find ourselves in the *bargaining* phase -- looking back, second-guessing our actions and decisions, wondering if we had done something differently, whether we might have seen different outcomes.

As we began to separate from the military, I distinctly recall being *depressed* about the new reality, feeling empty, withdrawn and unable to relate to others – a definite contrast to my usual way of approaching each day.

Acceptance of our new reality allowed me once again to start reaching out and reconnecting with friends and family. Acceptance does not necessarily mean you feel great, but at least you are better equipped to begin moving on and adapting to a "new normal."

As Kubler-Ross wrote, not everyone will experience major loss in the same way. You may find yourself feeling any number of emotions throughout your transition, beginning from the time you first recognize you are leaving military service until one day, you find yourself feeling content with your new reality. During this time, you may feel:

* Anxious or out of control
* A loss of identity
* Isolated
* Uncertain about where you belong
* Uncertain about how best to move forward

I hope you recognize that whichever or however many of these feelings you experience, you are not the only one feeling this way, even if the colleagues retiring alongside you are wearing broad smiles as they talk about the bright futures they see ahead. While the move into civilian life may not be difficult for everyone, there are many who, years later, still acknowledge they have not fully made the transition. It is definitely not a "one-size-fits-all" process.

Here are some important things to remember:

- No matter how foreign it may feel, it is not a sign of weakness to ask for help with processing your anxiety or with assessing how best to move forward in pursuit of a rewarding new purpose. Asking for help does not come easily to military leaders; the more senior the leader, the harder it is to acknowledge not knowing all the answers. No wonder it has been such an unspoken taboo to talk about the challenges associated with transition to civilian life.

- Don't hesitate to seek out trusted mentors who can provide an empathetic ear and serve as non-judgmental listeners with "no skin in the game." Every senior leader should have his or her own mentor; one is never too "senior" to benefit from an even wiser, outside advisor. It also can be helpful to speak with former colleagues who are often more than willing to share their transition advice and words of caution, based on their own experiences.

- Try to avoid feeling guilty about your struggles, while others with "greater problems" appear able to handle their own plight with relative ease. Avoid making such comparisons, since you are only viewing others externally. Successful transitions are going to mean different things for each person. Focus on your own challenges and opportunities and how you can achieve the goals you set in this next phase of life.

- Remember to keep channels of communication open with those closest to you during this time of change. Try to avoid the tendency to shut down or retreat into your personal "cave;" if you must enter, make sure it is only a temporary stay, not a permanent escape route.

- Be honest and recognize that transition may bring either a temporary or more lasting change in roles at home, with one partner becoming more decisive as the other needs more time to process the change and come to closure. It is important to take time to address this major life change and recognize that one's spouse also may be experiencing some struggles of his/her own.

As a retired Canadian admiral once told me:

> *I found the transition from uniform to "civvy street" a unique challenge, notably for the first six months. It reminded me of the sensation you get when stepping off a high-speed sidewalk. Mind and body must be prepared to adapt to the sudden deceleration or one can be thrown off balance. In retirement, the body adapts quickly to the slower pace, but the mind continues at three times the speed. Occupying much of this off-balance mental energy is the issue of identity and answering the question, "who am I without the uniform?" The process can be very disorienting, especially if these concerns are internalized. For those interested in starting work immediately after a military career, the transition from the moving sidewalk can be less dramatic, but can still be a challenge and put a dent in that "type A" personality and confidence.*

Skip, a former Master Chief Petty Officer of the U.S. Coast Guard, said:

The first hurdle was simply separating from an organization that I felt I knew literally from top to bottom. Retiring (from the military) was very difficult. You think you are preparing for it but when it happens, it is quite a shock. One moment you are involved in everything that the service is doing and the next moment you are totally out. It was a very hard pill to swallow.

The Coast Guard's famous motto is Semper Paratus which means, "Always Ready." Everyone has to leave the military eventually and while it is never easy, if you fully prepare for transition it will be easier.

Sometime back I was counseling a retired E9 who had never completed his college degree and had even let his security clearance lapse. To say that he had a difficult time in transition is a major understatement. Don't let it happen to you. Prepare for transition and you will be ready when the time comes.

*   *   *   *   *

OUT OF STEAM OR POWERED UP FOR TRANSITION?

Taking care of oneself, both emotionally and physically, is important for everyone. Too often, senior leaders put health matters on the back burner, due to perceived lack of time and the need to focus on other "higher priorities" associated with the job. As a result, many feel both mentally and physically exhausted as they wind down a long military career.

The transition period, from the time you begin the process through the immediate years that follow, is an especially critical time to focus on your emotional and physical well-being. Military Executive Health physicians often see an increase in depression, alcoholism, obesity, high blood pressure, insomnia and other ailments in senior military leaders after separation from military service. Some individuals experience marital difficulty and divorce or turn to drugs rather than acknowledge they are struggling to cope.

The reality is that your poor physical and mental health not only affects you directly, but also can have an impact on family relationships. Lack of patience, irritability, loss of interest along with declining physical well-being can cause excessive stress in even the strongest of families, creating alienation in place of a loving and supportive environment.

Exercise, regular medical checkups and good nutrition, as well as reaching out to others, become even more important as a way to deal with feelings of stress and anxiety, rather than keeping tensions and worries inside.

While on active duty, there may have been a need to keep things bottled up in order to fully focus on the task at hand, or to spare a spouse from some of the more traumatic experiences of military service. Now, more than ever, it is important to recognize the value of reaching out to others for additional support.

There is no cowardice in acknowledging a need for guidance and assistance; conversely, it is an act of true bravery. Being brave does not mean maintaining a stiff upper lip or stoic willingness to endure in silence. Quite the contrary, those who continually internalize their anxiety often mask a fear of embarrassment, rejection or loss of respect in the eyes of former colleagues. The brave act of asking for help and reaching out to others demonstrates your own humanity.

You now answer only to yourself and to your family, and are responsible for putting your well-being front and center before you can move forward, full-throttle, into your next life adventure. It is difficult to plow through with a positive attitude when you are in pain, either physically or mentally. You should not hesitate to consult a medical professional who can help diagnose how best to address your concerns.

*   *   *   *   *

TEN THINGS I WISH I HAD DONE DIFFERENTLY

While there are no do-overs in life, it can be helpful to learn from the lessons of those who have gone before. Since the transition process varies for every individual, each person will have a unique list of things that could have been done differently. Former senior military leaders I interviewed often said they wished they had done things differently in their own transitions:

1. *I wouldn't have taken the first job offer that came along simply because the employer told me how much he wanted me...I failed to consider whether I would actually enjoy doing the job every day, whether I could have gained a position that better used my talents or whether I could have gained a position with a better overall salary/benefits package than the job I took. I accepted the job because I was made to feel wanted. It helped me avoid the risk of rejection I was worried I'd experience in a job search.*

2. *It's important to demonstrate humility and a high energy level when you are in your 40s, 50s or 60s and potentially competing against younger, more eager competition for the same job. While those younger individuals may not have your military leadership background, they may in fact have more direct private sector experience and may be more familiar and energized working within the corporate culture.*

3. *Almost everything is negotiable when it comes to your benefits package, but I learned the hard way that knowing the when, what and whom to ask is critical.*

4. *There is no one correct model or pathway in senior military to civilian transition.*

5. *I didn't fully appreciate how challenging it would be to adapt to such a different workplace culture. I should have been more open to learning the company's culture, rather than trying to impose the way we did things in the military.*

6. *I should have started way earlier than I did and worked harder at building my network before, during and after the transition process ended.*

7. *Retiring to a place where you have no base or network is not a good idea.*

8. *I had no idea what I wanted to do; as a result, I had too broad a focus. This was not helpful either on the resume or during face-to-face networking.*

9. *Transition can be very stressful and it takes time and patience. For some it will be faster than for others, but I see many of my former colleagues more than two years after they retired from the military who have told me they still don't feel fully transitioned.*

10. *I wish I had taken the time to explore other possibilities beyond the federal government and the private sector. I might have preferred working in the nonprofit sector or teaching as a second career, but never really considered other options.*

*   *   *   *   *

FOCUS FORWARD

Your military service will always be a part of who you are. It has shaped your professional development as well as your personal growth over the course of your extensive military career. Most members of the U.S. Armed Forces would likely agree with the proud individual who calls him/herself a "Veteran Marine" rather than an "ex-Marine." Once a Marine, always a Marine; a similar message is understood within each of the other services.

One of the most powerful reasons that military service is so hard to leave behind is that you are leaving the team and the people with whom you belonged. It is difficult to replace the "we" with a new focus on the "I."

That said, your attention now must focus forward, rather than look back over your shoulder. Finding a new job, career or volunteer passion requires your full attention and energy. It may take some time before you feel able to maintain a steady forward focus; letting go of your military life with both your head and your heart is a critical first step in order to find a new place to belong. Even if your departure from military service was not your own decision, there is little to be gained by regret or second-guessing how things might have turned out differently.

Here are just a few of the broader questions you will need to address as you begin to focus on your own transition to civilian life:

- Do you and your family have specific limitations or desires that will dictate where you will live once you leave military life?

_____

_____

_____

- What are your financial needs going forward? Will you be able to live on your retirement income or will you need an additional income stream? What is needed to ensure that your lifestyle and emergency needs will be met?

  _____

  _____

  _____

- Are you and your spouse on the same page regarding professional and personal goals as you approach retirement years?

  _____

  _____

  _____

- Do you still have children in school or aging parents requiring personal and financial support?

  _____

  _____

  _____

- Are you looking for a short-term, no-stress job rather than longer-term opportunities to further advance your professional career?

  _____

  _____

  _____

The answers to questions such as these may directly influence your decision-making.

*　　　　　*　　　　　*　　　　　*　　　　　*

GETTING YOUR HEAD IN THE GAME

The days and months immediately prior to retirement from military service are often crammed with last-minute projects. Transitioning military members generally work hard to ensure a smooth hand-off to incoming leadership, complete final performance reviews and wrap up separation paperwork. But too many senior military leaders leave the process of focusing on their own transition until just a few months before it is time to retire, in part due to a sense of lingering obligation to their military service, and in part, perhaps because it is easier to focus on the details of the known versus the murky, unknown aspects of challenges that await.

As Tom, a retired O-6, notes:

(It's important to) discipline yourself to setting aside several hours each week to concentrate on the transition. Nearly everyone I know, including me, waited until the last minute. We are not ready to give up a connection with a service that we love! I felt some innate obligation to finish some projects and initiatives I had started. Once you or your service decide upon a retirement date, the top priority is finding a new job or, better yet, that next career.

No matter how busy your last years in military service may be, it is helpful to begin planning for the eventual transition into civilian life almost as soon as you step into a position of senior leadership. Focusing on transition does not mean you have given up on being promoted within your service. Instead, it reflects your recognition that you are the only one who can determine what comes next after military life draws to a close and that it will require dedicated, intentional focus that cannot wait until the day you remove your uniform. While some will retire on their own terms and by their own choice, others may find their transition necessitated by a missed promotion, avoidance of an objectionable assignment or mandatory retirement regulations. No matter the circumstance, leaving military service at some point is inevitable; post-retirement options should be contemplated, discussed and assessed sooner rather than later.

According to Jay, a retired Reserve O-7, transitioning military leaders must focus on education, preparation and networking that should begin well ahead of an expected separation date. Specifically, he advises:

- *Education: Take the transition courses; read and re-read a variety of transition books; learn civilian business language.*

- *Preparation: Research the industries of greatest interest to you and targeted companies within those industries; prepare and tailor your resumes; practice your interview techniques.*

- *Networking*: *Build your business network of classmates, colleagues, and family; use social media networking vehicles such as LinkedIn; actively engage key nodes of your network to learn more about the industries you've targeted, learn about job openings, become an advocate/messenger of your talent. The majority of jobs, especially for mid- to senior-level positions, are obtained through networking.*

Jay's advice for senior leaders who have had 20+ years in the military is to look for the next job/career that inspires passion – a job that will make you want to "jump" out of bed in the morning to get to the office. Too many think they need to find that job with the greatest financial compensation, only to find themselves miserable both at work and at home, adding unwanted stress and friction in both places.

*   *   *   *   *

FINDING A MATCH FOR YOUR SKILLS AND TALENT

There has been increased national focus on the importance of helping veterans enter the civilian workforce. Through efforts such as the White House's Joining Forces Initiative, it is widely recognized that veterans may need extra assistance to reintegrate successfully into civilian life.

According to a study released in 2012 by the Institute for Veterans and Military Families at Syracuse University, finding a job can be an important step for military members in transition:

> *One of the most significant issues facing transitioning service members...is the need to find and cultivate organizational attachments that replace the sense of belonging conferred previously through their attachment to the military organization....Not only does gainful and meaningful employment serve to provide economic stability throughout the transition period, but it also serves the purpose of creating a social support structure, important during the discontinuous life change represented by separating from military service.*

While you may not have given it much thought before, it is now important to conduct either an informal or formal assessment of your strengths, weaknesses, interests, and skills to help focus your personal and professional priorities.

- What aspects of your work, to date, have you especially

  enjoyed?

  _____

  _____

  _____

  _____

  _____

- What components of your job would you prefer to avoid

  doing in the future?

  _____

  _____

  _____

  _____

  _____

- What is your energy level, as you prepare to wind down your very hectic military schedule and career?

  _____

  _____

  _____

- Are you prepared to rev up your engines to acquire new skills and learn new content?

  _____

  _____

  _____

- Are you ready to learn and adapt to a new agency or corporate culture that is likely completely different from your former service's way of doing business?

  _____

  _____

  _____

  _____

- Will you need any additional education, credentials or degrees to be competitive with your military and civilian competition?

_____

_____

_____

_____

These are just some of the areas that require introspection, conversations with loved ones and discussion with trusted mentors and colleagues who have gone through their own military-to-civilian transition. The more you are able to understand your own motivations, specific skill sets, and how you can apply them moving forward, the better prepared you will be to express them to those in a position to support you.

*   *   *   *   *

LEADERSHIP IS ONLY PART OF YOUR STORY

One of my biggest disagreements with current military leader transition courses is the emphasis on the marketability of transitioning senior military members' leadership skills. This sets up a serious misalignment of expectations that benefits neither the military leader nor a prospective employer.

As a retired Army brigadier general, now a vice president at The Boeing Company, once said:

> *Senior leaders tend to oversell their ability to lead. I can find 100,000 leaders, so that can't be the only thing you are selling in an interview. Talk about your specific skills. For example, let the interviewer know you have a deep understanding of the federal budget process, who makes the decisions, how the decisions are made, when they are made, etc. I'd prefer to hire a person with skills like that, over someone who can only tell me that he/she commanded 50,000 people.*

It may come as a shock to many that their military leadership experience alone will not win them the civilian job of their choice. While employers often express an interest in military veterans' leadership capacity, the candidates ultimately hired are the ones able to highlight specific skills they possess to help prospective employers achieve greater success.

There are roughly a million individuals expected to leave military service in the next five years, either due to budget cutbacks, retirement or normal attrition. While many are junior-level members, there is no shortage of military leaders ages 45 to 60 who, along with their civilian counterparts, are joining you in the job market. Their resumes all include extensive leadership experience. Many also managed impressive financial and human resources throughout their careers.

Don't rely on your leadership experience alone to open the door to your next opportunity. For most senior leaders, finding the next path takes time, preparation and sound strategy.

*　　　*　　　*　　　*　　　*

DOES THE SHOE FIT?

If you've never held a professional job outside the military, it can be challenging to know in which other fields you might succeed. In an ideal world, transitioning military leaders would have the opportunity to do a paid six-month fellowship in a few areas of interest to help determine the best direction.

Imagine being able to shadow a private company's vice president, observing and contributing to the achievement of short-term corporate objectives. Alternatively, rolling up your sleeves during an emergency management fellowship with a local or state government could provide insights into public service closer to home.

Companies such as ExFederal.com provide an entrée into the contracting world by posting vacancies to which you can apply and make your resume available for full-time, part-time or short-term work as a contractor. Unlike choosing a long-term career, as you did in selecting the military, you can accept a contractor position and see if the work is a good fit for you.

Barring such short-term opportunities to see if "the shoe fits," there are other ways you can begin to assess the suitability of certain career paths.

The first method is to conduct a self-assessment; tools like this may help you make smarter civilian career choices. There are basically two kinds of tools – those that are self-driven and those that require interpretation by a licensed, trained professional. Some of the self-driven assessments may even be available online at no cost; however, they do not include analysis or evaluation of your results – there is no third party objectivity in the assessment.

Career self assessments, generally, are intended to give you greater insight into your interests, skills, personality and values. As a senior leader, you may feel you already have a strong handle on what you enjoy or dislike; nonetheless, you may find that your key motivators will change once you enter the civilian workforce.

Some of the more familiar assessment tools are the Myers-Briggs Type Indicator (MBTI) and the Strong Interest Inventory (SII) resource. Unlike the Myers-Briggs, the SII measures interests in four main categories or scales – General Occupational Themes, Basic Interests, Personal Style and Occupational Scales.

Career assessments also can be helpful to identify your strengths and other characteristics that make you stand out from your military and civilian competition. Tools such as 360 Reach enable you to use a third party to request input from current and former colleagues, bosses and friends; they are asked to complete a brief questionnaire aimed at assessing your rational and emotional attributes, their perceptions of your greatest strength and weakness and how you best engage in a team setting. There are free and fee-based options, though the analysis and evaluation typically demand a fee.

Another approach that can be pursued simultaneously is to connect with former colleagues and others currently working in areas of interest to you. These individuals are typically happy to share their experiences and perspective with those in the throes of the transition process. Here are the types of questions you may wish to ask:

- What do you enjoy most about your current job?

- What do you like least?

- What do you wish you knew when you first transitioned that you know now?

- What did you find most surprising about civilian culture?

- What can I do now to be more competitive in the interview process?

- How do you manage communications with seniors and juniors, including those who may be geographically dispersed?

- How is feedback provided at your company?

- If you could change anything in your workplace, what would it be?

- If you could redo your transition, would you have done anything differently?

Marci Alboher, author of *The Encore Career Handbook*, provides useful advice for transitioning military leaders interested in exploring alternatives to the traditional private sector/government routes, such as in the nonprofit sector. She highlights the importance of getting to know an organization to help determine the right fit:

> *Find some ways to get a closer look.*
> *Volunteer. Do an informational*
> *interview. Identify someone to follow*
> *around for an afternoon. Take on a*
> *pro-bono consulting project to test the*
> *waters. These kinds of experiences will*
> *help you pull back the curtain to see*
> *how the reality of a certain kind of*
> *work matches up with what you*
> *imagined it would be.*

Alboher points out in an interview with *Military Leaders in Transition* (www.seniormilitaryintransition.com) that members of the military might find comfort in a nonprofit environment focused on accomplishing a shared mission; at the same time, she advises that it is still important to find ways to get to know any new institution in which decision-making processes and hierarchy may be less obvious than they were in the military. She notes that cultures within the nonprofit sector, as within the private and public sectors, will vary widely based on an organization's size, management style, values and other factors.

*   *   *   *   *

PREPARING YOURSELF FOR SUCCESS IN A

DIFFERENT CULTURE

What is culture? How are we constrained by it? How do we adapt to a different culture in the workplace? Many senior military leaders may initially assume that, due to the diversity of assignments they have held and the multiple international and interagency collaborations they have facilitated, transition into a new workplace culture should be no big deal. They may assume they are being hired for their past accomplishments, their deep understanding of a given subject area and their familiarity with working within large organizations. These skills are definitely an asset, but senior leaders also must be prepared to spend the first several months on the new job adapting to a new way of getting things done.

As you step away from your military career to pursue a new position in government, the private sector or with a nonprofit or academic institution, take time to ensure that you are in a learning and listening mode, rather than a telling or directing mode. It is important to remain confident about your capabilities but, at the same time, let others know you recognize you still have a lot to learn. Demonstrate humility and your readiness to understand the organization, its culture and its people. Don't presume you are being hired to impose military structure, hierarchy and strategy onto a civilian organization unless that is what you are specifically told. Try to suspend judgment and take input from the new environment.

In transition to civilian life, everything changes. According to Dr. Sydney Savion, retired Air Force Captain and author of *Camouflage to Pinstripes*, military leaders in transition must leave behind the notion of "service before self." She notes:

(The) core values and beliefs of the military are very distinct from civilian culture. Therefore, when many military members reenter civilian culture, the stark differences they experience can foster doubt and conflict in the way they feel, think, and behave, as a result of being in a very dissimilar environment.

You are moving from a culture in which the lines of responsibility are much more clearly drawn as are the processes for accomplishing a given mission. The terms of engagement are well understood and well established.

Is it any wonder, then, that when the time comes to separate from the "we" after a long career in military service, it takes some time to find your place both as an individual and within a new organizational framework where you can again "belong?"

The culture shock may come a week, a month or several months later, when the military veteran realizes how different things are. Everything has changed except the military leader, who wonders what is broken with this new system and why everyone is doing things in what seems to be an ineffective, opaque, inconsistent – you choose the word – manner.

Be prepared to embrace:

- Doing more with far less, in many cases with no staff support and few financial resources.

- Being more self-reliant.

- The difference between the new, less formal organizational structure and the military hierarchical framework.

- Being comfortable with reporting to a boss who may be the same age as your son or daughter.

Mike Burroughs, a seasoned executive and author with an extensive background in global recruiting, executive coaching and organizational development, says that the question the prospective employer is pondering is not whether the retiring military leader can adjust to a new workplace, but rather *how quickly* he or she can make the transition.

Senior military leaders have much more to set aside and that is primarily the military culture and methods of getting things done; they are often quite different in the private sector. Even defense industry companies' cultures are quite different from the uniformed services. If a retiring senior military leader seeks a position within the government, the transition is less severe.

John Lees, career strategist and author of *How To Get A Job You'll Love* notes that:

> *The main challenges are about culture and language. The civilian work culture is very different – results are often obtained indirectly, often through persuasion and relationship building. Sometimes organizational results are as much about people as goals. The language issue is, however, central to transition. Everyone talks about transferable skills and expects that all you need do is list them in a resume, but the key to changing sectors is to describe your skill set in language that the decision maker can get excited about. This means talking to people in your target sector and listening to the way they describe top performers.*

Michael Watkins, author of the book, *The First 90 Days*, asked fellow members of the Harvard Business Review's LinkedIn group to share their perspectives on organizational culture. Here are some of my favorites from that discussion:

- *Culture reveals how things are done, reflecting the fundamental values and ethics by which an organization operates, as well as the perceptions and commitment of its staff.*

- *Culture can be classified into at least four types: **Group/Relationship Culture** (focused on teamwork and morale); **Developmental Culture** (rewards entrepreneurship and risk-taking); **Rational/ Process-Oriented Culture** (characterized by achievement and meeting goals) and; **Hierarchical Culture** (rewards rules, regulations and stability.)*

- *The culture of an organization is the sum of all the words and actions of all members. An organization's stated...culture may be captured in its vision, mission and values, but the actual culture is how people behave and speak at work.*

- *Organizational culture is "how we do it here."*

Daniel Pink, author of *To Sell is Human*, shares a very helpful exercise that he learned from Cathy Salit, owner of a company called Performance of a Lifetime. The exercise is called Conversation with a Time Traveler; it requires two individuals' participation. One plays the role of someone from the 1700s; the other thinks of a modern-day item, such as a traffic light or airport screening machine that would not have been in existence 300 years ago, and tries to explain it to the individual from the 1700s.

This is an excellent exercise to demonstrate how challenging even simple communication may be when a military leader enters the civilian workforce. The frame of reference is completely different, the language and acronyms are quite different, and the ways of doing business may seem completely strange and inefficient in comparison to how things were conducted in the military environment. It takes time to understand and learn the new culture and to work within it.

Salit says:

> *This exercise immediately challenges your assumptions about the understandability of your message…You are forced to care about the worldview of the other person.*

*   *   *   *   *

WHO DO YOU WANT TO BE TOMORROW?

Although you have held a variety of positions throughout your military career, you likely developed a set of specialties – engineering, aviation, combat arms, etc. Your path was set and to a certain extent, predetermined, based on those areas of specialization, along with flexibility provided by additional soft skills you picked up along the way. Some examples of soft skills are effective communication; team-building; ability to do more with less. In your transition, among the many questions you will need to address, are these:

- Do I want to be my own boss and start my own business? Am I ready (along with my family) to commit 24/7 to investing in the business and living without a reliable income stream, beyond my military annuity, in order to achieve a longer term goal? Do I have the resources and skills needed to get the business up and running?

_____

_____

_____

_____

- What about becoming a franchise owner? Would the proven business model and established framework provide the autonomy I seek? Am I comfortable with the risks involved? Which franchise excites me the most? Do I have the energy it takes to make it a successful operation? Do I have the resources I need to invest in a franchise operation? Do I enjoy personnel management, an important part of running a successful franchise? Would I prefer an owner-run or manager-run model? Do I know enough about the business of the franchise? Should I shadow a franchise owner in my particular industry of interest? (To learn more about franchising and discounted franchise fees and low-interest loans available to veterans, visit:

  www.franchise.org/Veteran-Franchise.aspx

_____

_____

_____

_____

- Would I like to work in the public sector for a civilian agency? At the federal, state or local level? Which of my current skills would be in demand? Are there jobs in those fields in the city or town where my family would like to live?

_____

_____

_____

_____

- Do I want a private sector position that might yield better overall compensation? What are the pros and cons of going this route? Am I prepared to devote my energy to strengthening a company's bottom line? Are there additional skills or certifications I need that would make me more marketable/appealing to a specific company of interest? What is my personal risk/reward calculation?

_____

_____

_____

_____

- Is being passionate about a new mission more important than financial compensation? What about a job in the nonprofit sector? Am I financially secure enough to accept somewhat lower compensation in order to do work that really excites me? Is my family in agreement about our financial needs, recognizing this means a lifestyle change at home?

  _____

  _____

  _____

  _____

- What about teaching? At the university, college, secondary or elementary school levels? Do I have the necessary degrees and credentials to be competitive for such a position? What about this path do I find particularly appealing? Is it the right fit for me?

  _____

  _____

  _____

- Associations and chambers of commerce represent a different avenue, whether at the local, state or national level. These organizations are driven by their memberships and may be focused on a particular industry or group of business leaders. Do I bring a particular expertise to an association that would be highly valued? Do I enjoy working as part of a committee to achieve goals? Am I comfortable promoting membership and helping to grow the association/chamber?

You may well have other questions. Your answers should take into consideration where you and your partner are willing to live, the standard of living you seek, desired work-life balance and the need for a regular paycheck to supplement your military retirement.

There are advantages and disadvantages tied to every path. You may make an initial decision based on how you are feeling immediately after separating from military service, only to find out within a year or so, that the choice you made was less than optimal.

Recognize that many who transition after a long military career may work in two or three different sectors or types of organizations before finding the right fit. Your main motivations may change after you have joined a new employer, helping you to reorient priorities. This does not represent failure; rather, it is one step closer to where you really want to be.

A retired U.S. Army Command Sergeant Major described his transition this way:

> *The ups included being mentally prepared; by that, I mean that I knew that when the uniform came off, so did the rank. I also knew where I was going to settle down and thus, started networking well in advance with several community leaders and businesses. As I thought about what came next, my goal was to find a job that provided fulfillment and teamwork.*

*   *   *   *

THINKING ABOUT RETIREMENT TO

THE GOLF COURSE?

While many will leave military service and seek out continued employment in another sector, some senior leaders may choose to leave the workforce entirely and retire to a community with an affordable cost of living. After working long days and being on call 24/7, some will fantasize about calling it quits and just living without the pressure of working.

While it is not uncommon for retiring military careerists to take some time off before jumping back into the job market, the decision to come to a full stop professionally is not for everyone. Life on the green may be a good choice for some; others may soon find themselves feeling underutilized, unfulfilled and lacking structure or purpose after just a few months on the golf course. It is not surprising to see several of these veterans soon resurface on LinkedIn or at other networking venues, subtly letting their former colleagues know they are ready to reenter the professional arena.

Transitioning senior military leaders who are not ready for full retirement but would like to explore a new direction without being driven by the level of compensation, may wish to explore some hybrid options. These might include any one or combination of the following:

- Volunteering for an organization close to one's heart, either in a hands-on capacity or as a board member.

- Bringing one's leadership, managerial, financial or administrative talents to an organization such as SCORE to help strengthen the capacity of small business owners.

- Pursuing an encore career that taps your personal or professional talents, such as becoming a master gardener, a mentor to young veterans or a lecturer on topics of interest for a community life-long learning program. (These types of avenues might be pursued as a volunteer or in some cases, might provide a small source of additional income.)

For those who decide to jump back more fully into the workforce, the sooner that decision is made, the better. The longer one has been out of sight, the harder it can be to get back in. It requires intensive effort, networking, and increased visibility within targeted communities of interest. The more intentional and persistent the outreach, the greater the likelihood these individuals will have a successful reentry. Each person must determine which path will bring the greatest fulfillment both in the short term and in the long run.

Those contemplating scaling back from full-time employment should consider questions such as:

- Do I have the financial means to live comfortably for the remainder of my life without additional employment?

  _____

  _____

  _____

- Will I be happy on the golf course (or woodworking in my shop or insert your preferred hobby here) for the next several years?

  _____

  _____

  _____

- Do I have my own, as well as shared, activities of interest with my spouse/partner? How does my decision to retire affect our relationship and our day-to-day life together? Will I achieve greater happiness and fulfillment if I stop working?

  _____

  _____

  _____

*   *   *   *   *

NETWORKING NITTY-GRITTY

No conversation about transition is complete without someone bringing up that pesky word "networking." What does it take to become a successful networker and what does that really mean?

Tired as you may already be of hearing everyone talk about the importance of networking, there is no getting around it when it comes to the job search. You may have some preconceived notions about networking and are thinking deeply about how to avoid it. After all, who really enjoys getting out there to make conversation and ask favors of people you don't really know?

Let's start by identifying what networking is and what it isn't.

NETWORKING IS NOT:

- Putting on a fake smile and shaking the hands of as many strangers as possible at a networking event.

- Handing out or collecting so many business cards that you may be mistaken for a blackjack dealer at the local casino.

- Meaningless conversation or a one-way request for a handout or favor from a former colleague or stranger.

NETWORKING IS:

- Building and sustaining relationships.

- Filling the well before you are thirsty.

- A two-way process through which you will offer help to others as they help you.

- **The most critical component of your job search and your continued professional success!**

Networking takes time and continued effort. It requires a thoughtful, open approach to rekindling stagnant relationships, building new ones and finding ways to be as helpful to others as you would like them to be to you.

There is no secret to the fact that the majority of jobs today are not found through newspaper or online employment ads, but through word-of-mouth networking. Networking is not a process that can be avoided – it is a job-searching fact of life. Networking also is an ongoing process that must be continued even after you have landed a civilian job. Staying connected with your professional network keeps you visible and top-of-mind for other opportunities that might be an even better fit for you in the civilian workforce.

Building and sustaining a network will best be accomplished using a multi-pronged strategy. It will include:

- Face-to-face conversations with friends, neighbors, current and former colleagues and family members. Letting these individuals know you are beginning a new job/career search and the kinds of things that interest you will help others keep you in mind when they learn of relevant openings.

- Participating at a variety of networking events, including career-related events sponsored by national or local chapters of military/veterans organizations such as the Military Officers Association of America (MOAA) or the Armed Forces Communications and Electronics Association (AFCEA) as well as at events targeting industries or organizations of potential interest to you in your next career.

- Reconnecting with former classmates in college and graduate school alumni groups. Many of these individuals may be working in fields of interest to you and may be more than willing to share their insights with former classmates.

- Using social media such as LinkedIn to connect professionally with former, current and prospective colleagues who share your fields of interest, as well as prospective employers in the public, private, nonprofit and academic sectors. (See next section for more about social media.)

- Seeking informational interviews to help you learn more about an industry or particular field of interest and to further expand the breadth of your network. Such conversations also provide a great opportunity to practice your interview skills, including the ability to concisely articulate the areas and types of opportunities of greatest interest to you.

- Ensuring you make at least one contact per day throughout your transition and beyond in order to grow and strengthen your professional network.

It is important to dismiss the idea that networking is asking strangers for favors or that it requires you to continually brag about yourself. You do have to be able to articulate the fields/professions that are of interest to you and to describe your strengths. It is equally important to demonstrate an earnest desire to be helpful to others, even if the ability to assist others may be further down the line.

*   *   *   *   *

GET ORGANIZED AND DO YOUR HOMEWORK

You may be inclined to think that getting out and meeting people over coffee or at events is an informal process that simply requires putting on a suit and marking the dates on your calendar. The more thoughtful and formalized you are in planning your conversations, identifying the individuals you would like to meet and the companies or organizations you would like to explore, the more productive your efforts will be.

It is equally critical that you establish a workable system for keeping track of your outreach and contacts. It does no good to collect a pile of business cards at a networking event only to discard them casually on your desk without immediately making notes about the conversations you had and those that require follow-up.

- Get organized with a methodical and intentional strategy that begins while you are still in military service.

- Do your homework ahead of time about the people you plan to meet or the organization or company you are interested in. If you are still a member of the U.S. Armed Services, check with your ethics advisor to remain in compliance with legal obligations before you reach out to any private sector representatives, to avoid any conflicts of interest. Your legal/ethics advisor remains an excellent resource even after you leave military service.

- Have some clarity about areas of specific interest so you can make the most of the limited time you will have to articulate your job interests with others.

- Keep track of all contacts, persons, companies, government agencies and other organizations of interest. Consider using an Excel spreadsheet or online tools such as JibberJobber.com that allow you to stay on top of each relationship, record next steps, action dates, etc. Don't let contacts fall through the woodwork or get lost among the many business cards you collected at the last event you attended.

- Prepare your pitch – the 30 second, one-minute and two-minute versions of who you are and what you hope to do to help others in your next job.

- Build relationships, reconnecting with dormant contacts as well as making new ones through informational interviews, joining LinkedIn groups, joining professional associations of interest, local chambers, etc.

- Don't confine yourself to your "silo" of current and former military colleagues; get involved, online and face-to-face, with groups and associations connected to prospective second careers.

- If you are interested in working for a particular company, join its LinkedIn group. Follow the company on Twitter. This is not creepy – you are instead showing the employer that you are doing due diligence.

- Locate YouTube videos featuring thought leaders from your target companies, including CEO comments to shareholders at annual meetings, to learn more about what's on the minds of corporate leadership.

- Increase your visibility – online, within key associations, etc. Think about how you can participate in LinkedIn group discussions on topics in which you have something valuable to contribute. You may decide to submit an article to a key journal on a topic in which you have expertise or write an op-ed for the local paper. Be sure to keep your comments professional and remember that your words, opinions and perspectives give employers insights into who you are professionally and, in some ways, personally. At the same time, this kind of effort will help to establish your expertise outside your current circles.

*　　　　*　　　　*　　　　*　　　　*

FINDING A JOB IS A FULL-TIME JOB:

WHAT'S YOUR STRATEGY?

It has been a long time since you were last completely responsible for finding yourself a job. The military has largely been taking care of that for you; the task is now solely in your hands. The process can vary greatly from person to person, and will be influenced by your visibility outside the military, specific skills and experience, geographic flexibility, salary expectations and most important, your ability to contribute to the new company or organization in the future.

As you advance your career in the civilian workforce, you may find yourself in a different job every two or three years; changing jobs is often required to attain a bump in salary or an increase in responsibilities. This is more the norm than the exception. Understanding this fact at the outset can help you better weather unexpected job shifts in the first few years of your military-to-civilian transition.

There are a rare few who are fortunate enough to receive an offer, before leaving military service, with a great pay and benefits package, the desired level of responsibility and autonomy, and the added bonus of working with a great team. More often, transitioning leaders may be approached by prospective recruiters or employers with lowball offers or jobs with higher degrees of risk than may be suited to your temperament or skill set. Not everyone will feel comfortable, for example, taking a position that requires selling a product or service back to his or her former military branch, even if the potential compensation is great.

Most senior military leaders will find that landing a new job and, more important, the right job, takes time. Be prepared to make a few missteps along the way – you may not necessarily be able to identify a good fit when you assess that first job offer. If things don't work out after a year or so on the job, try not to view this as a personal failure, but rather as a detour on the road to where you eventually will land. You are in uncharted waters and need to be resilient; your goal is to pursue an opportunity that will be a better fit.

Research shows that up to 40 percent of externally-hired leaders "fail" within the first 18 months on the job. This may be for a variety of reasons, including:

- The new hire was unable to adapt to the existing corporate culture.

- The company did not provide effective "on-boarding" for the new leader, who would have benefited from more than familiarization with simple corporate administrative procedures.

- There was a misalignment of expectations or miscommunication about goals and objectives.

While there are no crystal balls to help avoid making sub-optimal choices when it comes to the first post-military job, taking responsibility for doing your homework, actively networking, speaking with former colleagues and doing other research are all well within your control. Even with this active commitment, it can take many months in the current economy to land a position that is right for you.

*   *   *   *   *

USING A RECRUITER TO FIND A JOB

The idea of finding a job on one's own can feel overwhelming. Going to career fairs, meeting people for coffee and attending networking events take so much effort; who has the time or the inclination for all that? Your first instinct may be to let a recruiter do the work for you.

As Mike Burroughs, Managing Director at Sheer Velocity, points out:

> ***Don't think you can rely on executive recruiters to place you.*** *98 percent of your job search work will be personally researching and reaching out to people from whom you can learn and who might also be able to open some doors for you. There is a prevailing misconception in the marketplace, even among many executives with no military experience that executive recruiters are available to serve transitioning managers the way accountants or lawyers might also serve them. This is not the case.* ***Executive recruiters work for the clients they represent and their search assignments vary, based on their clients' needs at any given time.***

There are two main types of recruiters paid by the hiring company. The first is a contingent recruiter who is paid once a candidate is hired. Contingent recruiters typically fill jobs with salaries below $125,000. Contingent recruiters normally do not have exclusive listings.

In contrast, retained recruiters are usually paid an upfront fee and a hiring fee. These firms typically help employers fill executive-level positions with salaries usually above $125,000 and often are highly selective about the candidates with whom they will work.

Some firms take on both contingent and retained clients. Almost all recruiters operate in very high-stress environments and may be far less responsive to you as the job seeker than they will be to the company that has hired them. Again, this is because contingent and retained recruiters do not work for you; they work for the employers who pay them to find the best candidates.

There are specialized placement firms who will take you on as a client for a significant fee (which can range from $7,000 - $30,000), but most will eventually find a placement for you. It is incumbent upon you to do your homework and carefully research any firm that is charging you such a fee to ensure it is a legitimate and ethically-operated business.

Most executive recruiters have areas of specialty and maintain their own bank of potential candidates for the industries and fields they address. They may already know the leading candidates in a given field and how to find them when there is a position to fill.

If you wish to dedicate yourself to increasing your visibility with these kinds of recruiters, you will need to be strategic, persistent and patient. Specifically:

1. You will need to make sure you have a well-constructed LinkedIn profile that is updated regularly. More and more, recruiters are finding new candidates online.

2. Raise your visibility by joining LinkedIn groups related to your industries of interest and participate in discussions in which you have expertise. Recruiters frequently monitor these conversations and take note of those who are most relevant and thoughtful in the group.

3. Contribute articles to blogs and other publications; participate in industry conferences in fields of interest to you.

4. Ensure that your written and online presence highlights your greatest strengths and what benefits you bring to a prospective employer (beyond "leadership".)

Finding a Good Recruiter on Your Own

As with most things, word of mouth or referrals can be very useful. Ask former colleagues who have worked with a specific recruiter about their experiences and if they would refer you. You also may want to scour industry publications in the fields of interest to you for names of well-respected firms. You might find recruiters through professional associations or at industry conferences. There are a variety of recruiter directories, many of which are available online. Two examples are the Directory of Executive and Professional Recruiters (www.recruiterredbook.com) and the Association of Executive Search Consultants' International Executive Search Directory.

If you decide to initiate contact with a recruiter, you can send your resume along with a brief cover letter noting your compensation requirements, geographic flexibility and the specific talents you bring to the industries in which the recruiter specializes. Remember these individuals are extremely busy and unless your package stands out from the rest, this could be a long and relatively unproductive process to undertake. You also might request a 30-minute meeting with the principal to present your resume and explore possible fits.

Should you decide to build a longer term relationship with a recruiter, remember it is a two-way street. The more helpful you are in sharing useful and timely information and referrals to the recruiter, the more likely the recruiter will get to know you as a solid contact worth nurturing.

You will want to avoid contacting your recruiter more than once a week, so you don't become a nuisance. These individuals are working many relationships at once and may be less responsive than you expect, no matter how senior a position you previously held.

There are other factors to consider before signing an agreement with a recruiter. These include:

- Assessing the credentials and the track record of the firm in placing individuals with similar experience to your own and the firm's experience in your target sectors.

- Confirming up front the feasibility of working with more than one recruiter at a time, since each will have its own areas of specialty; at the executive search level, some may prefer not to work with you if you are not willing to use a given firm exclusively.

- Determining what happens if you reach out to a prospective private employer on your own, meet with company representatives and receive an offer. Will the recruiter still expect to receive its placement fee even though you did all the legwork?

- Reaching out to a prospective private employer on your own, letting the prospective employer know you are working with a specific recruiter and having the employer shut down any further conversation. This may happen when a company prefers to avoid paying significant recruiter placement fees on top of the salary and benefits package the company must already pay to the person filling the position.

*   *   *   *   *

I'LL DO ANYTHING BUT SALES

Most military leaders do not think of themselves as salespeople. In fact, there is a tendency to hold at arm's length former colleagues now selling back to their former military branch, with the view that selling in this manner is unseemly.

John, a retired Reserve O-8, whose own career included stints at PepsiCo, Booz Allen Hamilton, and the Department of Homeland Security, reminds us that:

> *Everyone is in sales... The reality is that virtually any company willing to pay you will have the expectation that:*
>
> - *You'll understand the company's business and products/services;*
>
> - *You'll represent the company in a conscientious and professional manner and;*
>
> - *When the opportunity arises, you won't pass on the chance to make a sale (or at least refer a lead to someone else who can make the sale.)*
>
> *That's part of the private sector bargain.*

Daniel Pink, author of *To Sell is Human,* tells us that our general distaste for sales stems from a time back in history during which the salesperson always had the upper hand, holding all the knowledge and therefore, all the power. Access to the Internet and global information has helped to even things out, allowing consumers greater ability to evaluate products and services independently in the marketplace.

Pink also dispels the notion that only extroverts can be great sales people. He tells us:

> *New research out of the Wharton School shows that the very best salespeople are not strong extroverts. But they're not strong introverts either. Instead they're ambiverts. That's a term that has been in the literature since the 1920s and it describes people who are in the middle — who are somewhat introverted and somewhat extroverted. Why are they more effective? Because they're more attuned. They know when to speak up and they know when to shut up. They know when to push and when to hold back. The good news: Relatively few of us are strong introverts or strong extroverts. Most of us are ambiverts, which means that most of us can be reasonably good at sales in all its dimensions.*

The truth is, no matter what your style, you have already successfully sold many concepts, directives, and ideas, to your children, your spouse and especially to colleagues on the job. When you persuaded others to adopt or change a policy, support a proposed budget or endorse a strategic plan, *you were selling*.

Selling Yourself as the Best Candidate for the Job

Selling yourself, initially, may feel somewhat unnatural, especially coming from an environment in which it is all about the team. At the same time, it is critical to remember that in the job hunt, you are your own best salesperson; you must be able to "sell" what you can do for a company or agency, so that they will want to hire you. Don't think of "selling yourself" as bragging; you are simply conveying important information about your talents and potential in a way that helps you stand out as the best candidate for the job.

Do you have your sales pitch ready?

The 30-Second Pitch

You have likely heard it said that you must prepare your 30-second elevator pitch since that may be all the time you have for self-introduction before the elevator doors open and your audience departs. The main point is that, whether it is 30 or 60 seconds or even two minutes, it is important to be able to briefly let someone know who you are, what you do, and how you plan to bring your talents to help a new organization…become more effective, save money, make money, grow, achieve its mission, etc.

Not only do people have a short attention span, you do not want to be in the position of monopolizing someone's time at a networking event when there are others still waiting in line. You need to be succinct and memorable. While it is important to briefly highlight past achievement, it is even more essential to address how you will build upon your previous experience to deliver tangible results for them in the future.

Here's a to-the-point approach that you can adapt to reflect your own background and experience:

> *I have a solid academic background in aviation and management, with an undergraduate degree from Embry Riddle and an MBA from Wharton. Over the course of my military career, I have overseen flight operations for six military bases around the globe and led a reorganization of a wing that resulted in $1.5 billion of savings for the Air Force. I am interested in bringing my talents in operations and management to help an aviation company increase its competitiveness in the global marketplace.*

Telling Your Story

Daniel Pink credits a former story artist at Pixar Animation Studios with creating a template for another kind of effective sales pitch you might think of using next time you are asked about your greatest achievement. The "Pixar Pitch" is based on a story-telling structure that could be adapted to tell your own story; it involves six sentences that flow from one another:

Once upon a time_____. Every day,

_____. One day,_____

_____. Because of that,

_____. Because of that,

_____

_____. Until finally, _____.

If one of my transition clients were to use this "sales pitch," he might tell his "story" this way:

After 9-11 (Once upon a time), the United States declared war on Al Qaeda and the Taliban to combat global terrorism. One day, the U.S. Army was asked to establish bases quickly in Afghanistan to enable U.S. military operations in support of its stated mission in the region. Because of that, we needed to set up operations in the absence of formal policies to drive the process. Because of that, I helped developed the first-ever DoD policy for forward-operating contingency bases, covering the entire life cycle from planning, design, construction, operations, and management, through closure or transfer of the base to host countries. Until finally, this policy was signed and is currently being implemented, yielding greater uniformity and efficiency in the way we set up contingent bases around the world in support of our global military operations.

Give this tactic a test run to sum up your greatest achievement. Don't forget that you can maximize the impact of your story if you can use it to *highlight the talents you will bring forward* (beyond leadership) to help a prospective employer achieve greater success.

What will your story say?

_____

_____

_____

_____

_____

_____

_____

_____

_____

_____

*   *   *   *   *

STANDING OUT AMONG YOUR MILITARY AND

CIVILIAN COMPETITION

After many years of thinking as part of a "collective" focused on a shared mission, your new focus is to identify and be able to articulate what makes *you* the one deserving of a desirable position. Talking about yourself may not have been encouraged during your military career, so it may take some time for you to highlight succinctly the talents you bring to a prospective employer. You will need to give serious thought to the following questions you can expect an employer to ask:

- Why should I hire you instead of one of your military

  colleagues?

  _____

  _____

  _____

- Beyond your obvious leadership experience, what specific

  skills do you have that can help my agency/company/

  organization achieve greater success?

  _____

  _____

- Give me an example where you guided a program or project from conception to completion.

_____

_____

_____

_____

_____

_____

- How well do you understand the specific challenges facing our company and our industry? What talents do you bring that will help us meet those specific challenges?

_____

_____

_____

_____

_____

It may be helpful to gather input from past bosses, colleagues and direct reports who are willing to give you frank perspective on your unique strengths and best talents. You can do this on your own or through more formalized processes. Be careful, however, about cutting and pasting verbatim language from past performance reviews when describing your skill set on a resume or in your LinkedIn profile; these should not sound as though written by a third person.

*   *   *   *   *

DEVELOPING YOUR PERSONAL BRAND

When you wore your military uniform, it is likely that the first word used to describe you was your rank or pay grade – Master Chief, Colonel, General, Admiral, etc. It was not only a title but also a large part of your identity. Now that you are no longer wearing that uniform, try this exercise: Write down five to ten words that best describe who you are, how people view you and what colleagues most value about you and the work you have done. Now ask five other people – perhaps your spouse, your last boss, past staff members and a couple of neighbors – to write down their own five to ten words that best describe you. You may be surprised to learn what others view as your stand-out qualities are not necessarily what you think they are.

There has been much talk in recent years about creating your own personal brand. Erik Deckers and Kyle Lacy describe a personal brand as the emotional response people have when they hear your name. In their book, *Branding Yourself*, they encourage readers to ask themselves:

- *What do I want to be known for?*

- *What qualities do I want people to associate with me?*

- *What is the first thing I want to have pop in their heads when they hear my name?*

The authors remind us that branding, as self-promotion, is not bragging about one's self – a trait unnatural within the military community. A personal brand simply tells people who you are and what you do. There are many tools you can use to promote yourself and help you stand out from the crowd in your job search. These include:

- Your resume

- Your LinkedIn profile, LinkedIn groups and content of your LinkedIn discussions

- Other social media such as Twitter and Facebook

- Articles, opinion pieces or guest blog posts you write

- Key messages you deliver in face-to-face conversations

- Your business cards

The key is to maintain consistency in content and in the case of print materials, such as a paper resume and business cards, some visual consistency as well. Your efforts must be ongoing, since your target audience may not see the message the first time you deliver it.

Collectively, these things will help shape your brand and the world's view of who you are and how you differ from the countless other applicants competing for employers' attention. Your brand must be clear enough to paint a picture that remains etched in the minds of those you encounter, whether you are leaning toward work in the public, private or nonprofit sectors.

*   *   *   *   *

DO YOU SPEAK SOCIAL MEDIA?

While it may feel somewhat foreign to be sharing professional information about yourself online, it is virtually (no pun intended) essential to a successful job search. Recruiters and employers are regularly using social media to find suitable and interesting candidates for key positions; if they can't find you, you will be at a serious disadvantage.

The most useful professional social media tool to use is LinkedIn. There are several valuable social media guidebooks on the market about making the most of LinkedIn and other social media resources, but here are a few of the essentials you need to know right at the start.

According to Joshua Waldman, author of *Job Searching with Social Media for Dummies*:

> • *You absolutely must get good at using social media. It is the number one skill for winning both the job search as well as in your (next) career. There are enough statistics to show that most companies rely on social media, and some rely on social media almost exclusively.*

- *Before jumping into the pool, dip your toes. Figure out your personal positioning. Who are you? What motivates you? What problems are you able to solve for the companies you are targeting? Answering these questions first will make your use of social media more effective.*

- *Be bold. Companies are looking for employees who know how to be flexible and navigate change. By embracing social media, you demonstrate that you are agile and open to change. When you use social media boldly and with integrity, you really stand out. You're not just easier to find, you become the obvious choice.*

- *Don't wait for prospects to find you. You have to figure out where your prospects are and then go to them. Make sure you have a 100% complete profile on LinkedIn. Be sure to include relevant and important information in the Projects, Skills, Publications and Certifications areas, as well as your level of clearance.*

Military leaders in transition may want to think carefully before putting clearance data into a LinkedIn profile, though you will want to include it in your resume.

Make every effort to solicit a handful of recommendations (versus endorsements) from former bosses, colleagues and direct-reports. A brief paragraph from individuals in each of these groups helps to shed light on what makes you a stand-out job candidate and, unlike endorsements, are written by individuals who are very familiar with your strengths and areas of expertise.

Veteran recruiter Joe Turner (www.JobSearchGuy.com) cites a recent survey of U.S. hiring managers, noting that 66 percent used LinkedIn to find candidates for job openings, 23 percent used Facebook and 16% used Twitter. As a result, it is important to keep your online presence professional and appropriate.

Google yourself to look for any negative information; there should be no compromising pictures of you or raging rants filled with expletives. You may think you have deleted something that was somehow saved somewhere else before you removed it from your profile. Be cautious and thoughtful about what you put out there because prospective employers are very resourceful and will search your background carefully. Keep it clean. If you can't delete it, be prepared to defend it.

*   *   *   *   *

SUCCESS IN YOUR NEW MISSION

One of the key messages throughout this book is the importance of not looking back over your shoulder, or dwelling on past achievements and stature. In order to reach a new peak in your life – and indeed, there can be more than one – you have to keep your focus forward and demonstrate to the world what you want to accomplish as you take on new opportunities.

Michael Watkins, author of *The First 90 Days*, offers one of the best blueprints for every leader seeking to excel in a new organization. His must-read book outlines key transition challenges such as the need to:

- Promote yourself: Watkins advises leaders to avoid assuming that what has made a person successful up to this point in one's career is what will continue to make that person successful moving forward. *The dangers of sticking with what you know, working extremely hard at doing it, and failing miserably are very real.*

- Accelerate your learning: *Getting acquainted with a new organization can feel like drinking from a fire hose. You have to be systematic and focused about deciding what you need to learn and how you will learn it most efficiently.*

- Match strategy to situation: *A clear diagnosis of the situation is an essential prerequisite for developing your action plan.*

- Secure early wins: *In the first 90 days, you need to identify ways to create value, improve business results, and get to the break-even point more rapidly* – the point at which you become a net contributor of value to your organization.

- Negotiate success: *You need to figure out how to build a productive working relationship with your new boss and manage his or her expectations...Crucially, it means developing and gaining consensus on your 90-day plan.* Remember that your boss may be significantly younger than you, but with more direct experience in the company or organization. His or her priorities may be very different from what you think they should be; your success will be tied to understanding your boss' frame of reference.

- Achieve alignment: *bringing an organization's structure into alignment with its strategy.*

- Build your team.

- Create coalitions.

- Keep your balance: *The risk of losing perspective, getting isolated, and making bad calls are ever present during transitions...The right advice-and-counsel network is an indispensable resource.*

- Expedite everyone: *Help everyone in your organization accelerate their own transitions. The quicker you can get your new direct reports up to speed, the more you will help your own performance. Beyond that, the benefits to the organization of systematically accelerating everyone's transitions are potentially vast.*

*   *   *   *   *

CONCLUSION

As you transition from military life, keep these 10 key points in mind:

- Transition will be different for each individual. It can be a brief or long-term process and will be influenced by many factors, some of which are outside of your control.

- Be brave and seek the assistance you need, whether it be from a medical professional, spouse, executive career consultant, recruiter, mentor or former colleague.

- Be proud of who you are and what you have achieved, but focus on what it is that you can do for a prospective employer going forward.

- Be able to outline what makes *you* the one to hire over the rest of your military and civilian competition.

- Leadership is not your only story.

- Balance your expectations; passion for your new job can be as important as the pay.

- Remember that selling is something you have done throughout your personal and professional life; the first thing you must sell to a prospective employer is yourself.

- Hubris is not your friend. Demonstrate your willingness to continue learning and your flexibility to adapt to a different culture, no matter how senior a position you held while in the military. Suspend judgment and be willing to take input from your new workplace.

- Networking is essential before, during and after a job search. Stay visible and engaged and continue to do what you can to help others professionally and personally.

- Be patient and recognize that transition can feel like a roller coaster ride. You are not alone, even if others wear a better poker face.

- Stay positive and keep the channels of communication open to others who stand ready to help you achieve success in your new mission.

*   *   *   *   *

HELPFUL RESOURCES

Books

Alboher, Marci, *The Encore Career Handbook: How to Make a Living and a Difference in the Second Half of Life.* New York: Workman Publishing, 2013.

Burroughs, Michael, *Before Onboarding: How to Integrate New Leaders for Quick and Sustained Results.* Amazon/Kindle edition

Deckers, Erik and Kyle Lacy, *Branding Yourself: How to Use Social Media to Invent or Reinvent Yourself.* Quepublishing, 2013

Goldsmith, Marshall with Mark Reiter, *What Got You Here Won't Get You There.* New York: Hyperion Books, 2007.

Hay, Mary, Lani Rorrer, James Rivera, Ron Krannich and Caryl Krannich, *Military Transition to Civilian Success.* Manassas Park: Impact Publications. 2006

Krannich, Ron and Carl Savino, *The Military to Civilian Transition Guide.*

Kubler-Ross, Elisabeth, *On Death and Dying.* New York: Simon & Schuster/Touchstone, 1969.

Lancaster, Hal, *Promoting Yourself.* Simon & Schuster/Free Press, 2002.

Pink, Daniel H., *To Sell is Human: The Surprising Truth about Moving Others.* New York: Penguin Group, 2012.

Savion, Dr. Sydney M., *Camouflage to Pinstripes: Learning to Thrive in Civilian Culture.* Dallas: Brown Books Publishing Group, 2012

Sherman, Dan, *Maximum Success with LinkedIn.* McGraw-Hill Companies, 2013.

Watkins, Michael, *The First 90 Days: Critical Success Strategies for New Leaders at All Levels.*
Boston: Harvard Business School Press, 2003.

Online Resources

Career Enlightenment: www.careerenlightenment.com

Careerealism: www.careerealism.com

Glassdoor: www.glassdoor.com

LinkedIn: www.LinkedIn.com

Military Connection: www.militaryconnection.com

Military Leaders in Transition: www.seniormilitaryintransition.com

Simply Hired: www.simplyhired.com

The Ladders: www.TheLadders.com

Twitter: www.twitter.com

<u>Organizations</u>

Air Force Association: www.afa.org

American Legion: www.legion.org

Armed Forces Communications and Electronics Association (AFCEA): www.afcea.org

Association of the United States Army: www.ausa.org

Corporate Gray: www.corporategray.com

Disabled American Veterans: www.dav.org

ExFederal: www.exfederal.com

Irelaunch: www.irelaunch.com

Marine Executive Association: www.MarineEA.org

Milicruit: www.veteranscareerfair.com

Military Family Network: www.emilitary.org

Military Officers Association of America: www.moaa.org

Military Spouse Employment Partnership: www.msepjobs.com

National Chief Petty Officers Association: www.goatlocker.org/ncpoa

National Veterans Transition Services: www.nvtsi.org

Navy League: www.navyleague.org

Veteran Franchising (International Franchising Association): www.vetfran.org

Government Agencies/ Resources

Joining Forces: www.whitehouse.gov/joiningforces/resources

Make the Connection: www.maketheconnection.net

Military OneSource: www.militaryonesource.com/transition

The National Resource Directory: www.nrd.gov

Tricare for Retired Reserve and Families:

www.tricare.mil/Welcome/Eligibility/NGRRandFamilies.aspx

Tricare for Retired Service Members and Families:

www.tricare.mil/Welcome/Eligibility/RSMandFamilies.aspx

USA Jobs: www.usajobs.gov/veterans

Made in the USA
Charleston, SC
15 March 2014